A PRINCE OF
THE CHURCH

A PRINCE OF THE CHURCH

Schleiermacher and
the Beginnings of
Modern Theology

B. A. GERRISH

FORTRESS PRESS   PHILADELPHIA

Library of Congress Cataloging in Publication Data
Gerrish, B. A. (Brian Albert), 1931–
　A prince of the church.

　(The Rockwell lectures; 1981)
　Bibliography: p.
　Includes index.
　1. Schleiermacher, Friedrich, 1768–1834—Addresses, essays, lectures.
　I. Title. II. Series.
　BX4827.S3G47 1984　　230'.044'0924　　83-48924
　ISBN 0-8006-1787-8

K107L83　Printed in the United States of America　1-1787

To H. H. Farmer 1892–1981
and Wilhelm Pauck 1901–1981

Best of Teachers

Contents

Preface   11

1. Religion and Reflection   17

2. The Christ of Faith   35

3. The Acts of God   51

Sources   71

Index   77

Imagine the concern for religion and the scientific spirit united, for the sake of theory and practice, in the highest degree and in the most perfect balance, and you have the idea of a "prince of the church."

Schleiermacher,
Brief Outline on the Study of Theology

Preface

Ever since I first began to appreciate the "father of modern theology," as Friedrich Schleiermacher is commonly called, I have wanted to present his ideas in a form that might show their worth beyond the limited circle of professional theologians. In a summer conference for ministers at Union Theological Seminary in Richmond, Virginia (1971), I tried to indicate the place of his Christology in the wider story of Protestant thinking about Christ; and I tried again before a largely undergraduate audience at Valparaiso University (Miller Lectures, 1973). Work on my contribution to Cambridge's *Religious Thought in the Nineteenth Century* then convinced me that it would make much better sense not to isolate Schleiermacher's estimate of Christ from his idea of God, since he himself expressly points out why the two must be held inseparably together. His theology is not a circle with one center, but more like an ellipse with two foci.

My first endeavor was completely recast in this twofold form, with an introductory statement on what Schleiermacher understood theology to be, in a summer school for ministers at St. Olaf College (1979). But the version presented here was occasioned by my Rockwell Lectures (1981) for a town and gown audience at Rice University. Material from the third Rockwell lecture was used again in the third of my Tate-Willson Lectures (1981) at Southern Methodist University on "*Anima Mundi:* The Debate about God in Goethe's Germany," a theme I am presently developing into a study of the pantheism, atheism, and so-called divine things controversies. Finally, the three lectures were brought back together once more as the Anderson Lectures (1982) at the Presbyterian College in Montreal.

To the patient midwives who have helped me with their en-

couragement and criticism I am immensely grateful, and especially to Professor Niels C. Nielsen, Jr. and his colleagues at
Rice University. Schleiermacher experts may feel that from all
this labor only a mouse has been born. They will miss the usual
apparatus of an academic monograph and may judge my theme
to be much too general. I am not insensitive to the perils, of an
extramural introduction to any field of specialization; and I
dare say I would hesitate to send these lectures out if I were not
able to point fellow scholars to my other publications, in some
of which I have offered more sharply focused studies on
Schleiermacher with as many learned notes as anyone could
reasonably ask for. But I must add that I have never regarded
lectures to nonspecialists as merely a popularizing of conclusions established within the walls of one part of the academy;
they are rather a challenge to the academics to see how far they
have really gotten their ideas clear, and whether they know their
whole subject well enough to go straight to the heart of the matter. This is the challenge I have at least tried to meet. There is, of
course, another kind of introduction: anyone who wants an
overall review of Schleiermacher's career and literary produc-
tion cannot do better than to turn to Martin Redeker's *Schleiermacher: Life and Thought*, translated by John Wallhausser
(Philadelphia: Fortress Press, 1973).

It has been said that theology, unlike other university dis-
ciplines, faces its real extramural test in the pulpit, not in
another lecture room. That may very well be so. Schleiermacher
himself was a preacher as well as a professor, and he has shown
to many seekers, in his own day and since, that it is still possible
to be both devout and intellectually honest. My interpretation
takes him to be exactly a two-sided "prince of the church."
These three lectures, however, *are* lectures: they serve the ends
of understanding, not persuasion. Unfortunately, educated persons who are otherwise well informed about modern views of
the human species and its environment, and who are perfectly
aware that knowledge in many fields has made immense strides

since the Middle Ages, may know little about the progress of modern theology. Perhaps they feel no great need to find out more; they may suppose that faith (to borrow Martin Luther's translation of 2 Thess. 3:2) is not everybody's thing. But for those who do want to know more, or at least for some of them, my hope is that these lectures may in some small way help to fill the gap.

There is another gap of understanding, within the Christian community, between Schleiermacher's (conscious or unconscious) followers and his (conscious or unconscious) opponents. The opponents do not share his deep conviction that modern habits of thought demand radical theological change, a thorough overhauling of the meanings traditionally ascribed to Christian language. The consequent polarization of the church into conservative and liberal parties, and the lack of trust and respect between them, is one of the major weaknesses in the contemporary religious situation. I suspect that in our day, as in Schleiermacher's, many devout believers at first find his ideas shocking, or would if they heard about them. But I would be very glad if these lectures helped some of them also to understand him, or to understand him better, and so to recognize that he began where they begin.

My own appreciation of Schleiermacher was a long time coming. The first essay I wrote on him, in seminary, concluded triumphantly with a damning quotation from Karl Barth: "One can *not* speak of God simply by speaking of man in a loud voice." Barth's *The Word of God and the Word of Man*, which a friend gave to me, looked much more like the powerful rhetoric of John Calvin, my first theological hero, than did the unfamiliar thickets of Schleiermacher's world; and I lent a ready ear to the widespread rumor that Barth's "neo-orthodoxy" had dealt the deathblow to Schleiermacher and liberal Protestant theology. And yet it was my good fortune to have two outstanding teachers who thought the news of Schleiermacher's demise premature. Things had come to such a pass, H.

H. Farmer used to tell his students at Cambridge, that he could
no longer get to sleep at night until he had looked under the bed
for Schleiermacher. Wilhelm Pauck, too, withstood the tide,
and he announced a seminar on Schleiermacher just at the end
of my student days at Union Theological Seminary, New York.
Still unconvinced, I did not sign up for it. Only in meeting my
teaching responsibilities a few years later did I discover the
founder of modern Protestant thought for myself. I dedicate
this little book to my teachers as an act of penitence from a slow
learner; or, rather, I dedicate it to their memory, since one died
shortly before my Rockwell Lectures and the other shortly after.

In preparing the lectures for publication, I have not attempted to alter the general style of the spoken word. But I
could not resist the temptation to make numerous changes,
many of them slight but some of them substantive. A few
statements that might mislead on their own have been provided
with refinements which could have lost an audience but should
pose no difficulty to a reader. However, the character of this introductory study remains the same, and a keen-eyed reader may
even detect where insertions have been made.

I owe a special debt of thanks to two good friends who read
the typescript and gave me the benefit of their comments and
criticisms: Schubert M. Ogden, a theologian who knows his
Schleiermacher, and Joseph T. Ledwell, a pastor who knows
the men and women (myself among them) who face him each
Sunday from the pews. I have, of course, tried to do justice to
all their suggestions for improvement. But I must absolve them
from any responsibility for the defects of this little book and not
take their encouragement and help to imply agreement with
Schleiermacher or my treatment of him. I recognize, in particular, that on two issues they raised—the parallel between
Christian dogmatics and Christian ethics in Schleiermacher and
the opposition between Schleiermacher and Barth—a great deal
more could still be said.

My thanks go also to Rehova Arthur, once again, for her

faithful work on my manuscripts. And for preparing the index and reading the proofs I am grateful to Mary Jean Kraybill.

More by accident than design, but still appropriately, these lectures now appear during the year when scholars are commemorating the 150th anniversary of Schleiermacher's death.

The University of Chicago   B. A. GERRISH

1. Religion and Reflection

> What is the real place of those dogmas and doctrines that commonly pass for the sum and substance of religion? . . . [Concepts are] nothing but the communal expression for a determinate feeling. Religion, for its own sake, has no need of this expression, scarcely even for the sake of communication. But reflection needs it and creates it.
>
> Schleiermacher, *On Religion:*
> *Speeches to its Cultured Despisers*

Friedrich Schleiermacher (1768–1834) is not an easy thinker. One of his contemporaries, Claus Harms (1778–1855), gave an intriguing account of reading the *Speeches on Religion* for the first time. Since Harms became a leader of the confessionalists and an opponent of Schleiermacher, it is remarkable that he could look back on the event as the hour in which his higher life was born: he received from the book, he said, the impulse of a movement that would never cease. But it was not easy going.

> It was Saturday about noon. In the afternoon I began to read, having told my attendant to inform everyone who might call that I did not wish to be disturbed. I read far into the night and finished the book. After that I slept a few hours. On Sunday morning I began again from the beginning, read again the whole forenoon, and began again after dinner; and then came a sensation in my head, as if two screws had been clapped upon my temples.

So Harms put the book down and took a walk. Apparently, he thought the double migraine was well worth it. But other first readers of Schleiermacher may wonder.

WHY SCHLEIERMACHER?

Students of religious ideas may recall the pain of their first exposure to Schleiermacher, especially if they were required to

follow the usual route through the second speech and the introduction to *The Christian Faith*. The first appearance of the
Speeches on Religion (1799) is commonly said to have in-
augurated the modern period in religious thought, and the second speech, on the nature or essence of religion, is no doubt the
most important; in it, Schleiermacher offers his famous definition of religion as a feeling—a sense and taste for the infinite.
But the second speech is full of dense, convoluted, and obscure
paragraphs that are apt to intimidate first readers. It is, in fact,
not only the most important speech but also the most difficult
of the five.

Schleiermacher's great theological treatise, *The Christian
Faith* (first published in 1821–22), is similarly judged to be a
work of epoch-making significance, to be ranked with the *Institutes* by John Calvin (1509–64) as one of the masterpieces of
Protestant thought. But it, too, is a formidable challenge to first
readers, and some of the most difficult sections appear already
in the introduction. In particular, the third and fourth sections
of *The Christian Faith*, in which Schleiermacher again locates
religion or piety in feeling, not in knowing or doing, and distin-
guishes it from all other feelings as the feeling of absolute
dependence, are so densely packed and couched in such elusive
language that one can stare at them a very long time without
much sense of enlightenment. Even the tough Scots who translated the book apparently hesitated over some of the centipede
words in the original German, and to be on the safe side they re-
tained them in parentheses along with the best English
equivalents they could manage. Many students must have spent
hours mesmerized by those two short sections, their sense of
panic growing as the deadline for their first Schleiermacher
essays drew inexorably closer, and they must have finally laid
aside their heavily underlined texts and turned anxiously to
some approved secondary help instead. And there may have
been an additional reason, besides the shortness of time, why
they could not generate the special effort required to read

Schleiermacher: for a while, thanks largely to Karl Barth (1886–1968), his reputation was at a low ebb. Would the effort have been worthwhile?

Barth was one of those readers, like Harms, whose first look at Schleiermacher brought an instant sense of excitement and discovery. During his student days at Berlin, he bought a copy of the *Speeches on Religion* and responded to his initial reading with a grateful "eureka," even entertaining the view (so he said) that these were the most important and correct writings to appear since the closing of the New Testament canon. But he was later disillusioned. He confessed in his last written statement on Schleiermacher that he could see no way from him to the great tradition of the Christian church, and he insisted, at least provisionally, that a choice had to be made. "For the present," he wrote in 1968 when very little future was left to him, "I can see nothing here but a choice."

During the middle third of the twentieth century, Schleiermacher was not a very fashionable theologian. To say he *went* out of fashion would hardly be the right way of putting it, as far as the English-speaking world is concerned. Schleiermacher's *The Christian Faith* did not appear in English until 1928, more than a hundred years after its first publication in German. Albrecht Ritschl (1822–89), by contrast, fared much better: the first volume of his massive work *The Christian Doctrine of Justification and Reconciliation* appeared in English in 1872, just two years after the first German edition, and the third, constructive volume of the work (first German edition 1874) appeared in English twenty-eight years later, in 1900. If Schleiermacher's *The Christian Faith*, not Ritschl's *Justification and Reconciliation*, is the true masterpiece of modern Protestant theology, the delay in putting it into English is astonishing. And I suspect one reason why the work was finally translated is that it had come under sharp attack from a new theological generation in Germany; the translation was not an unqualified compliment. Why, then, do I venture to speak about this difficult

and—as some would add—outmoded German theologian of the
nineteenth century?

The question could be fully answered only by a detailed
scrutiny of all Schleiermacher's leading themes and their per-
tinence to the current theological situation. I could, of course,
answer autobiographically, in terms of my own debts to him,
but that would be as inappropriate as the first alternative is im-
practicable. Instead, I offer three admittedly general, but not
subjective, reasons for an invitation to think about Schleiermacher; for the rest, my subsequent discussions of selected
themes will have to justify themselves as best they can.

First, no matter what the theological verdict one finally
decides to pass, Schleiermacher has a secure place among the
very few giants of Christian thought from whom theology will
always have to take its bearings. He belongs, in other words, in
the company of Augustine (354–430), Thomas Aquinas (1225–
74), Martin Luther (1483–1546), and Calvin; and it would be a
very un-Barthian thing to do if we added Barth himself to the
list but omitted Schleiermacher. Barth spoke of him as the
"great Niagara Falls" to which the theology of two centuries
was inexorably drawn, and he posed the question whether we
are really as free from his influence as we imagine. "Not until
E. Brunner in 1924," Barth said, "did anyone write against
Schleiermacher with presuppositions that were really different,
free from Schleiermacher." And he added mischievously in
parentheses: "Even if they were perhaps only relatively free
from Schleiermacher!"

Second, for all his difficulty and the uncompromising demands he makes on his reader, Schleiermacher merits attention
as preeminently a church theologian. He admits that he does not
do dogmatics in such a way that he can be used directly in the
pulpit; that, in his opinion, would be poor theology. Preachers
should be forced to think theology through first for themselves
and then put it into their own words. But no theologian has ever

insisted more emphatically that "the crown of theological study" (to say it in his own words) is *practical* theology. Ernst Troeltsch (1865-1923) went so far as to declare that Schleiermacher's dogmatics has a *technical* character, in the sense that anyone who masters its contents will understand the dynamics of the religious consciousness and so will possess the "technical" means to represent it and nurture it. And one of Barth's most important insights into Schleiermacher's work was that it needs to be understood in part from his sermons. In my opinion, a serious disservice is done to the father of modern theology if we persist in reading only his second speech and the introduction to his dogmatics (or two paragraphs from it).

I do not mean, of course, that Schleiermacher was on the side of the angels and therefore makes wholesome reading. But the second point does have to do with what one should expect from reading him, and with which readers one would therefore expect to profit most; and it seems very clear to me that in this respect, as in others, Schleiermacher has been misunderstood. He concerned himself with facts and phenomena—with real, live religion, not simply with "God" as a philosophical construct. He understood Christian theology to be (in his terms) "empirical," not "speculative." True, he had nothing against speculation; he even tried his own hand at it in his philosophical lectures. But he insisted that *theology*, if it is to be soundly based, must start from what is actually or factually given in religious experience, more particularly in Christian faith. He had the "religious studies" interest in the essence and forms of concrete religion and the church theologian's interest in the actual faith of Christians. Any aversion to him as merely academic or speculative must rest on a totally unwarranted inference from the occasional intricacy of his thought.

Third—and for myself this was the discovery that most demanded a change of mind—Schleiermacher was outspoken in his loyalty to the Reformation heritage. The accusation of the neo-orthodox critics was that he broke the line of succession running back to Luther and Calvin; hence neo-orthodoxy itself was sometimes termed "neo-Reformation" theology, as though it had picked up again the fallen standard of Protestantism. In actual fact, it must be said that the difference between Schleiermacher and Barth is a difference over what the Reformation heritage really is. And in the post-neo-orthodox decades of the twentieth century, we see the need for second thoughts about the nature of theological liberalism precisely as a development of Reformation theology.

Taken together, all three of these reasons for an invitation to Schleiermacher study suggest that we have to attempt a genuinely fresh look at him, one that will break the stereotype familiar during the heyday of neo-orthodoxy. But it should be added that at no time in the twentieth century, outside the neo-orthodox camp, has Schleiermacher been without his avowed or tacit witnesses. In the program of Rudolf Bultmann (1884–1976), for instance, Barth recognized a vigorous Schleiermacher renaissance. While he was scornful of the little men whom he counted among Schleiermacher's contemporary epigones, Barth respectfully named Bultmann as a genuine pupil of Schleiermacher, viewing him as one who stood in the great tradition of the nineteenth century. He did not approve of Bultmann's "demythologizing," of course; he believed Bultmann's program was a Schleiermacher renaissance because it repeated Schleiermacher's methodological errors, accommodating the Word of God to worldly wisdom and turning theology into anthropology—the study not of revelation but of human religiousness. Nevertheless, the later Barth also saw at least the possibility of revising his estimate of the father of modern theology and asking whether a theology of concrete experience might not claim after all to be authentically Christian as a theology of the Holy Spirit. We do not need to inquire here just what that might entail. The point is this: the need for reappraisal of Schleiermacher has found expression both inside and outside the company of his critics.

Schleiermacher's own rules of interpretation, laid out in his famous *Hermeneutics*, should have paramount importance to anyone who wants to take a fresh look at him. To understand a literary work, Schleiermacher held that one must first attempt to gain an overview of the whole. Hence, a book of more than trivial significance has to be read through before one backs up and takes a harder look at any individual part. The same, I think, holds true for a person's lifework. How can one possibly discover what Schleiermacher was about by staring mesmerized at two problem paragraphs in his systematic theology? One has to move on, even without fully understanding each individual point, especially with a highly systematic thinker for whom each part expressly has its meaning only in relation to the whole.

Schleiermacher also believed that a large part of the hermeneutic task is to grasp the author's intention. Now this rule, admittedly, has come under fire in recent years as an unjustifiable psychologizing of the interpretative task; and I am inclined to agree that it will not unlock every kind of literary text or exhaust all the treasures that a great classic has to offer. But it surely fits well the task of understanding *theological* texts by preeminently autobiographical thinkers like Luther or Schleiermacher.

I take the risk, then, of trying to get a broad perspective on Schleiermacher's work as a theologian. In the second and third lectures my assumptions will be that the whole of his theology can best be seen as moving between two points: a specifically Christian relationship with Christ and a universally human consciousness of God. However, by way of introduction, I want first to get at the experiential character of Schleiermacher's entire theological enterprise, since it is this, in my view, that contains the clue to reappraising him as a church theologian in the legitimate succession of Luther and Calvin. And this initial

assignment requires three things of me: to say something about
his life, to comment on the text I consider the best introduction
to him, and to suggest in conclusion how I think we might
classify him among the varieties of Christian theologians.

AMONG THE MORAVIANS

"Religion," Schleiermacher says in his *Speeches on Religion*,
"was the maternal womb in whose sacred darkness my young
• life was nourished." He was born into a devout family. His
father, an army chaplain, underwent a spiritual awakening
when Schleiermacher was nine; and five years later Schleiermacher, too, experienced a precisely datable conversion while at
school among the Moravians. His mother's confidence in the
protective Moravian community was apparently vindicated. She
had trembled for her children, she said, "considering the soul-
endangering opinions, principles, and habits that are so pre-
valent in the present times," but was reassured when they were
admitted to the Moravian school. She died shortly afterwards,
and Schleiermacher recalled her contented words: "Now that all
the children are going to the Brethren, I shall be of little more
use here, so I may as well lay me down and go to sleep."

The letters of Schleiermacher that survive from his years
among the Moravians are utterly fascinating. They are filled
with talk about the Savior's love, his own unworthiness, and
how he longs for a deeper spiritual experience. It is the standard
talk of the twice-born pietist—the "born-again Christian." But
• from the first there are traces of a certain diffidence. In later life
Schleiermacher recalled that even before he went to the
Brethren's school he had a peculiar thorn in the flesh, which
consisted in a "strange skepticism." In particular, he conceived
the odd notion that the whole of ancient history rested upon
spurious documents; but skeptical habits of mind overflowed to
other matters as well. For a time the devout community pro-
tected Schleiermacher from himself; and if he confessed to his
mother that he had not entered upon the full enjoyment of

grace, she wisely took his humility to be itself a work of grace in his heart. But worse was to come.

His spiritual troubles reached the crisis point only when he transferred to the Moravian seminary after his mother's death. In the short autobiographical sketch that he later wrote for the church authorities, he spoke of "companionship with Jesus," commended to him by his teachers, as something he longed for rather than had. Its cultivation, so it seems, was inhibited by the questioning spirit, which now began to assert itself within him, and he tried some outside reading not prescribed by his teachers.

In a letter to his father, Schleiermacher drops the mild hint that his teachers fail to deal with those widespread doubts that trouble so many young people of the present day. His father misses the hint. He has himself read some of the skeptical literature, he says, and can assure Schleiermacher that it is not worth wasting time on. For six whole months there is no further word from his son. Then comes the bombshell. In a moving letter of 21 January 1787, Schleiermacher admits that the doubts alluded to are his own. His father has said that faith is the "regalia of the Godhead," that is, God's royal due. Here is Schleiermacher's anguished confession:

> Faith is the regalia of the Godhead, you say. Alas! dearest father, if you believe that without this faith no one can attain to salvation in the next world, nor to tranquillity in this—and such, I know, is your belief—oh! then pray to God to grant it to me, for to me it is now lost. I cannot believe that he who called himself the Son of Man was the true, eternal God; I cannot believe that his death was a vicarious atonement.

The father's reply is terrible: his insensate son has crucified Christ, disturbed his late mother's rest, and made his stepmother weep. The cause of his straying is ambition for the honors of the world. And so the father solemnly disowns his son: "I must, for you no longer worship the God of your father, no longer kneel at the same altar with him." Yet the poor man

cannot quite bring himself to leave it there. He ends: "I can add
no more except the assurance that with sorrowing and heavy
heart, I remain your deeply compassionate and loving father."

I wish we could trace the story further and in detail. But we
cannot delay; and as it happens, some of the crucial documents,
available to Wilhelm Dilthey (1833–1911) when he worked on
his Schleiermacher biography, have unfortunately been lost.
The one point I want to make is this: if we did trace the story to
its conclusion, we would have to decide that what Schleiermacher lost was not his faith in Christ but his first understanding of it. The sufficient evidence for so deciding is, indeed,
his masterwork, *The Christian Faith*, in which orthodox doctrines are criticized and yet everything still hangs on the picture
of the Savior and its compelling attraction. As Barth rightly said
(in the language dear to the pietists and evangelicals), Schleiermacher had a "personal relationship with Jesus that may well be
called 'love.' " Hence, we are not surprised to learn that, although he dropped out of seminary and attended for a while the
now rationalist University of Halle, a reconciliation with his
father eventually took place.

In 1790 he took his first ordination exam, and on 16 August
1791 he wrote to his father the cheering news: "My heart is
properly cultivated . . . and is not left to wither under the
burden of cold erudition, and my religious feelings are not
deadened by theological inquiries." Notice how he puts it: there
is a contrast between the religious feelings of the heart and the
cool reflection of the intellect, but they can, apparently, very
well live together. And in 1802, when his father was no longer
living, Schleiermacher paid a return visit to the community of
the Moravian Brethren and wrote the famous words:

> Here it was that for the first time I awoke to the consciousness of
> the relations of man to a higher world. . . . Here it was that that
> mystic tendency developed itself, which has been of so much im-
> portance to me, and has supported and carried me through all
> the storms of scepticism. . . . And I may say, that after all that I

have passed through, I have become a Herrnhuter [Moravian] again, only of a higher order.

THE CHRISTMAS DIALOGUE

By the time those words were written, Schleiermacher had already achieved some distinction as author of the *Speeches on Religion*. The contrast between feeling and intellect, which begins to emerge as the cardinal point in our thoughts about him, could very well be illustrated from the second speech. There he argues that doctrines are not the essence of religion but simply the result of reflection upon religious feeling. It is absurd to think of a belief as mere acceptance of what somebody else says; each of us must rather see with his or her own eyes, and then our beliefs will be genuine expressions of our religious feeling.

Instead of looking more closely at the *Speeches on Religion*, however, I want to turn to an admittedly less-momentous little piece, entitled *The Celebration of Christmas: A Conversation*. In the most recent English translation, it runs to no more than sixty pages. But it is quintessential Schleiermacher in both thought and style. It is the closest he ever came to writing the novel one of his friends proposed to him, and it is perhaps the most pleasant and painless introduction to the fundamental theological shift that he brought about.

He wrote the "Christmas dialogue," as it is commonly called, in the three weeks before Christmas 1805, intending to present it to his friends as an anonymous gift. In Germany it was, and still is, the custom to distribute presents on Christmas Eve. Sometimes they were left untagged, except for the name of the recipient, so that everyone might have the fun of guessing from whom the gifts came. Hence, Schleiermacher's own Christmas present—the dialogue itself—was given anonymously. Actually, he did not allow the printer enough time, delivering the last pages of the manuscript to him on 24 December, and the book was not published until January. But that made no difference to its character and intent.

The scene of the Christmas dialogue is the drawing room of a middle-class German home, gaily decorated for the occasion. To begin with, it is simply the actual fun of Christmas that occupies us: the opening of presents, the singing of songs, the exchanging of family news, and the sheer delight of companionship. Then, as the casual conversation develops, three themes are subtly interwoven.

The first theme is music. The inspiration for the Christmas dialogue first came to Schleiermacher on his way back from a flute concert. Music played an important role in his life, and it also plays an important role in the dialogue. One of the guests proposes the view that music is a more basic medium of religious expression than the spoken word. May one perhaps find here the solution to a problem, that religious feeling seems to have been choked by the spirit of the age? Perhaps music can release it again.

Some of the music is provided by Sophie, the daughter of the host and hostess, a rather improbable child with wisdom beyond her years. She informs the company that she would have liked to include a rainbow in her nativity scene, seeing that "Christ is the true surety that life and joy will never more perish in the world." (She is a *very* precocious child.) By means of Sophie, the theme of musical expression passes over into a second theme: the simplicity of childhood, without which it is impossible to enter the kingdom of God. But is not childishness something we must someday grow out of, leaving the charm of illusion behind us? Here Schleiermacher's literary skill finds the bridge to his third theme.

The hostess, Ernestine, remarks that there is a difference here between the sexes. Men cannot come to terms with childhood, although in some respects their behavior is a perennial extension of childhood: they never grow up, but remain little boys at heart. Hence, for them maturity is always a struggle. For women, on the other hand, the transition is less unsettling, since their life already lies implicit in the games of their childhood.

Schleiermacher means, I am afraid, homemaking and nursing dolls—not what a twentieth-century feminist thinks of as a woman's destiny. And there is more to come.

The third theme is feminine nature. This is just as much authentic Schleiermacher as the theme of music. He was a great admirer of women, possibly for all the wrong reasons, but for now that is not the point. He even confessed freely that he would have liked to have been born a woman. (The psychologists must judge what to make of that.) Initially shy in the presence of the opposite sex, he turned his shyness into something like awe and then gave his awe a cosmic interpretation: it was the mysterious force of the feminine that made his world go around. He would have agreed with the concluding mystic chorus in Johann Wolfgang von Goethe's (1749–1832) *Faust*: it is the "eternal feminine" that draws us upward. Why? Well, partly because women, to Schleiermacher's romantic way of thinking, had a unique advantage over men in the capacity to penetrate intuitively to the heart of things. This put women on the side of religion as he understood it, and he expected the cultured despisers to recognize this important point, to which he alludes in the *Speeches on Religion*. But he also expected Christian women to recognize that in public they should exercise the remarkable power of their feminine nature only indirectly, through its control over the persons of their husbands. This was the lesson he discovered, or thought he discovered, in the Scriptures, and he made it the subject of an interesting sermon on the fifth chapter of the letter to the Ephesians.

Marriage and the family were thus the proper embodiments of Schleiermacher's thoughts on womanhood. He was by nature "the marrying kind," as we say. A very interesting contrast, incidentally, with Luther, who seems to have married chiefly because Katie was left over when all the other local nuns had found husbands. A contrast, too, with Calvin, who only married because his friends assured him it was a good thing to do, and who never quite grasped the difference between a wife and a

nurse. But that is another story. In the dialogue, Schleiermacher's admiration of women takes on a somewhat sentimental expression that is not to everyone's taste. There are bio-
graphical reasons for this. He had just received final word from
the woman he loved that she would not marry him, and he was
mooning over it. Her decision was probably a wise one, since
she was already married to a Lutheran pastor. But she had kept
Schleiermacher hoping for several years, and this helps to explain the rather syrupy opening of the dialogue.

As the guests enter, it is the figure of the hostess that draws
every eye.

> She it was in whom at first they all delighted. . . . The child hug-
> ged her knees and gazed wide-eyed at her—unsmiling, yet with
> infinite charm. Her lady friends embraced her, and Edward [her
> husband] kissed her beautiful downcast eye; and they all, as be-
> came each of them, gave her evidence of their hearty love and
> devotion. She herself had to give the sign for them to take
> possession [of their presents].

It sounds like something from a glossy-covered magazine for
lonely hearts. But Schleiermacher was grieving over the
domestic bliss that had eluded him. He got married later, for-
tunately, but to someone else.

The second and third sections of the dialogue—after the
initial section on music, childhood, and womanhood—are
strongly contrasted with each other in style, and in a sense they
continue the third preliminary theme. The women deeply move
the company as they take turns relating Christmas reminis-
cences. The men, by contrast, nearly ruin the party by starting a
high-powered theological argument about the meaning of the
incarnation. I want to return to the shape of the men's argument in my second lecture. For now, I only emphasize Schleiermacher's obvious point: the men really do come close to ruining
the party, arguing about the reliability of the four Gospels and
about the historical Jesus, the meaning of redemption, essential
humanity, and so on.

While the men are going hard at it, another guest quietly comes in late. But when invited to join the argument, he bluntly refuses. He is shocked at the terrible turn the Christmas celebration has taken with this highbrow debate among the men. Christmas for Joseph, the latecomer, is "one long, loving kiss that I have given to the world." He wants to know if Sophie is still awake to put the celebration back on the right track with cheerful singing. And so the sophisticated discourse gives way to the emotional, even erotic, talk of a sentimental piety, and the party ends up at the piano.

What is the meaning of the Christmas dialogue? In part, it lies in what the men actually say in their heady discourses. But that is not all. I may even have made the point too obvious in my selective summary. It is this: theological reflection, however necessary, makes sense only if it is framed within a life of spontaneous piety, since, when all is said and done, theology is nothing other than honest, persistent, critical reflection upon piety. The nonverbal communication of music, the direct and spontaneous perception of a child, the intuitive awareness of a woman, and the uninhibited effusiveness of the pietist—all of them in Schleiermacher's mind stand for the immediacy of genuine religion. He sets them in sharp contrast to the restless, analytical, critical spirit of the masculine mind. And yet the two contrasting types belong as inseparably together as male and female: there *must* be reflection in the Christian family, but it makes sense only if it is contained within a life of genuine and spontaneous piety. Piety, after all, is the actual object of theological reflection.

A LIBERAL EVANGELICAL

My concluding point is a short one. I simply want to propose a suitable label for what Schleiermacher was about, and I do not believe I can do better than revive an old label, which no longer has much currency in the present day. In his *History of Christian Doctrine*, which first appeared in 1896, George Park Fisher

(1827–1909) called Schleiermacher "the founder of the school of liberal evangelical theology." That, I think, is exactly the right description: it says much the same as Schleiermacher's own description of himself as a "Herrnhuter [a Moravian, a pietist] of a higher order."

Whatever the complexities of his writings, and I admit there are some, the program he set himself was in essence very simple. The clue lies in his distinction between feeling and intellect, intuitive piety and reflective belief—not as antagonistic but as correlative, like female and male. It was well said by A. E. Biedermann (1819–85) that Schleiermacher was the "regenerator of modern theology" exactly because he combined depth of feeling and acuteness of intellect in such an unusual degree. These two sides of our humanity are not the same, but they belong together (along with action or doing). Because they are not the same, we can say that what Schleiermacher lost in the Moravian seminary was not his religion but a system of doctrines. And because they belong together, it is possible to conceive of his theology as simply the turning of his critical intellect upon the content of his religious sensibility, not to destroy it but to understand it and give it a more adequate form. More exactly, in Schleiermacher's Christian ethics *(Sitten-lehre)* the intellect attends to the evangelical consciousness as it issues in a special way of behaving, and in his dogmatics *(Glaubens-lehre)* it attends to the evangelical consciousness as it issues in a special way of believing. Together, these two enterprises make up the substance of his theological program.

The program was "evangelical" because it was the distinctively evangelical Protestant consciousness (his own) that Schleiermacher made the object of his inquiry; it was "liberal" because he did not consider himself tied to the old expressions of it. I know that these days evangelicals are usually considered conservative by definition, so that a "liberal evangelical" may sound like a contradiction in terms. But it has not always been that way. An evangelical in England, like a pietist in Germany, was once a champion of experiential religion against the dead weight of traditional forms. And the Germans, at least, have never forgotten that "evangelical" is the badge of continuity with Luther and the Reformation. Interestingly, it was with an appeal to Luther that Schleiermacher confirmed his insistence on the priority of faith over reflection. "Was it not the case with our Luther," he asked, " . . . that his theology was manifestly a daughter of his religion?" Perhaps, after all, it is not a contradiction but a redundancy—a piece of needless repetition—to say that Schleiermacher was a *liberal* evangelical. That, historically speaking, is exactly what an evangelical originally was.

2. The Christ of Faith

The original activity of the Redeemer is best thought of as a kind of invasive activity that is nevertheless embraced by those it works upon as an activity that draws them to itself, since they turn toward it by a free movement—just as we ascribe a power of attraction to anyone to whose formative influence on our minds we surrender ourselves willingly.

For us, however, the influence of his community takes the place of his personal influence, because the picture of him that is still available to us in the scriptures owes its origin and perpetuation to the community. My proposition thus rests on the assumption that the community's influence in producing the same faith [as Jesus did] is simply the influence of the personal perfection of Jesus himself.

Schleiermacher, The Christian Faith

One of Schleiermacher's keenest critics, D. F. Strauss (1808–74), correctly understood his man when he wrote that *The Christian Faith* really has but one dogma, the dogma of the person of Christ. I shall need to qualify this judgment later, in the third lecture, but I have no doubt that it rightly informs us where to make our next beginning—exactly there where the previous discussion broke off. Strauss clearly perceived that what Schleiermacher looked for in the gospel story was the picture, impressed upon him by his education among the Moravians, of the personal Savior with whom a relationship of love is possible. This is precisely what we would by now expect, unless, and this did not in fact happen, Schleiermacher's progress had taken the form of renouncing his youthful faith. In turning from the general relationship between religion and reflection to a specific dogma, we can also anticipate, up to a point, the direction his thoughts about Christ would need to follow.

FAITH AND FORMULAS

The doctrinal world of Schleiermacher's boyhood and youth collapsed while he was at seminary, not because of unsound instruction received from his teachers, who were theologically orthodox, but in part because he did some outside reading of his own. And when, after weeks of anxious hesitation, he summoned up the courage to share his distress with his devoted father, the father judged that his son's doubts cut at the very heart of Christian faith. The verdict was not surprising: his son could no longer bring himself to confess without hedging that Jesus of Nazareth was the true, eternal God or that in dying he bore the punishments owed by others and not by himself. I dare say most of those who today wear the badge of evangelical Christians would be as quick to condemn the young Schleiermacher's doubts as was his father.

But what Schleiermacher in the long run was not able to doubt was the blessing he had actually received from the Savior, particularly in the Moravian community. At first he quit seminary and took up the study of philosophy at the University of Halle. At least, reading the philosophers was how he actually spent his time; his father supposed he was furthering his theological education, only now in a more dubious, liberal university. Remarkably, however, the detour into the far country led the prodigal home again. The piety of his youth sustained him through the crisis of belief, and he could finally make his marvelous confession that he had become a Moravian again—of a higher order. But as the phrase "of a higher order" indicates, it was not quite the same person who came back home.

How then had he essentially changed? The clue lies in the distinction he learned to make between living religion and its doctrinal expression. Doctrines are not propositions one has to believe on pain of eternal damnation; together with outward actions, they are ways in which the religious community externalizes the piety by which it lives. Hence there can be no final, permanently binding doctrinal formulas. On the contrary, it must always be the duty of the church to test the adequacy of its doctrines to its inner life. Are the creeds and confessions, the preaching and the teaching of the community still fit vehicles today of the faith that once produced them?

Schleiermacher embarked on persistent, probing criticism in the candid recognition that old creeds may become antiquated, and yet he supposed that his encounter with God and Christ remained constant through the ceaseless quest for more adequate forms of expression. To our ears, there may be a hint of presumption in styling oneself "a Moravian of a higher order." But elitism was not characteristic of Schleiermacher. In making his case against rationalist and speculative theologies, he refused to admit that his faith was any different from the faith of other Christians, including unspeculative and unphilosophical Christians. As his open letters to his friend Friedrich Lücke (1791–1855) make clear, the only difference of "order" he could admit in the church was a matter not of faith but of the ability to explicate and awaken it.

In form, all Schleiermacher's theological or, better, dogmatic work was an inquiry about the adequacy of doctrines to the faith they represent. And if we want to turn next to some of the ways in which he undertook to rethink individual doctrines from the inside out, I do not think there can be any hesitation over where to begin. Strauss was right: it is "Christology"—the doctrine of the person of Christ—that dominates Schleiermacher's theological reflection from beginning to end. His first doubts had to do with the person and work of the Savior, and the final version of his great systematic work, *The Christian Faith*, was determined throughout by his effort to put Christology on a new footing. Christian faith, he tells us there, is distinguished from all other faiths, even from those monotheistic faiths with which it has the closest family resemblance, "by the fact that everything in it is related to the redemption effected by Jesus of Nazareth." "There is no other way of participating in the Christian community than through faith in Jesus as the Redeemer."

Schleiermacher's thoughts on Christology had to be developed, however, partly through reappraisal of inherited ideas. Strauss was not mistaken in calling Schleiermacher's Christology "the really positive element" in *The Christian Faith*, but the positive construction called first for criticism. The purpose of the criticism, as Schleiermacher himself informs us, is to hold the church's christological formulas to strict agreement with the Christian self-consciousness, as he believes himself to have rightly analyzed it. The question, then, is this: How far do the formulas fit the analysis in essentials, and how much of them in detail had better be given up as imperfect, unessential, or misleading?

The motive behind the posing of the question is not only intellectual but also practical. If, as we shall see, Schleiermacher finds himself compelled to put a very low estimate on the official christological formulas of the church, that is largely because he judges them of little actual use to the church: they cannot give any guidance, he says, in rightly preaching Christ. The church needs formulas that can be presented to Christian congregations in religious instruction, and the truth is that even the most orthodox divines when they preach must set aside the traditional ecclesiastical definitions and find a language that can really contribute to strengthening a living faith. What Schleiermacher means is that no preachers are going to explain living faith in Christ by telling their flock that in Jesus Christ divine nature and human nature were combined in one person, or that in the Blessed Trinity there are three divine persons but only one divine essence. That just is not the way to do it. So, whatever other defects there may be in the old formulas, they seem to labor under the defect of a limited practical usefulness. They may be passed on for the sake of transmitting the letter of a dead tradition, but in the meantime the church's responsibility for preaching Christ may lack an adequate language.

To some extent Schleiermacher is echoing a sentiment of the Protestant Reformers. Luther, in particular, expressed strong doubts about the practical usefulness of technical trinitarian language, even of the term "Trinity" itself; and in an exposition of Exodus 12 (1525) he let slip this remark: "Christ is not called Christ because he has two natures. What is that to me?" But Luther and the Lutherans did not as a consequence attempt to revise the church's formulas, which are simply reproduced in Articles 1 and 3 of their Augsburg Confession (1530). It is perhaps not quite fair when Schleiermacher remarks that the Reformation did nothing for the christological dogma, but simply repeated old formulas. It could well be replied that Luther did something very significant: he filled the old formulas with fresh life. But at least it can be affirmed that an authentic Reformation motive lay behind Schleiermacher's quest for new formulas altogether. It was not the only motive, however, and it would seriously misrepresent his enterprise if we failed to list briefly three further reasons why he thought a fresh, critical look at the dogma of Christ was essential. All three reasons have to do with intellectual changes since the Reformation, although they no doubt had earlier roots.

THE DOGMA OF CHRIST

The old christological dogma had already been questioned in Schleiermacher's day simply on the grounds of its logical incoherence. He was not the first to criticize it; he inherited a tradition of criticism that had its modest beginnings in sixteenth-century Socinianism and culminated in the hostile, antichurch assaults of the Age of Reason. For the Enlightenment critics, the problem with the church's christological and trinitarian dogmas was not that they were religiously unfruitful but that they made no sense. And it must be admitted, with qualifi-

cations, that Schleiermacher thought the critics were right:
doctrinal revision, he believed, made urgent by the needs of the
congregations, was required also to extricate Christian theology
from a logical muddle.

In particular, he agreed that one must inevitably fall into
logical difficulties if one clung to the old formula "Two natures
in one person." The formula's intent was to assert two things
simultaneously: the existence of God in Christ and the Christian's brotherly communion with Christ. With this, says Schleiermacher, he agrees. But he argues that there must be a better
way to carry out the church's good intention, since the formula
is, and always has been, productive of endless confusion. Let
me mention just one of his points by which he thinks the orthodox dogma is reduced to an intolerable dilemma.

If Christ is one person formed out of two natures, does he
also have two wills? If we answer that he has only one will, then
we are forced to admit that either the divine nature or the
human was incomplete, that is, lacked a will. But if we answer
that he has two wills, then it seems impossible to maintain that
he is one person. In short, it seems to make no sense to speak
either of a nature without a will or of a person with two wills.
And the problem gets even more complicated, Schleiermacher
points out, when the dogma of the Trinity is introduced into the
discussion. Then we have to add to the puzzle of two natures in
one person the further puzzle of three persons in one essence,
the second of which is somehow identical with the divine nature
in Christ.

Schleiermacher makes the point in abstract logical terms. But
to verify that he is addressing a real problem, one needs only to
look at the writings of some of the early Christian fathers. Take
Tertullian (160?–220?), for example. In his writing against the
heretic Praxeas, he lets the activity of the Incarnate Word fall
apart into two separate series of activities. The divine nature, or
the Spirit, works the miracles, for instance, but the human
nature hungers, thirsts, grieves, and dies. Somehow, Schleier-

macher wants to affirm, against this hopeless christological schizophrenia, that Jesus of Nazareth was a real person; but he must do it without falling into the other error of reducing Jesus to a human body inhabited by a divine intelligence.

Here, then, is one added reason for christological second thoughts: the alleged collapse of the old "two natures" doctrine. (I say "alleged" because, of course, there were some in Schleiermacher's day who thought the doctrine could still be salvaged, as there are in our own day.) The second additional reason has to do with the fact that Schleiermacher's world had begun to ask questions about the relationship of Christianity to other religions.

Now here, too, is a problem that traces its roots all the way back to the early Christian fathers. But the fathers approached the problem in the confidence that Christianity possessed in Christ the highest revelation of God. They did not deny that fragments of divine truth could be found scattered throughout the pagan world, but they held that in Christ the divine wisdom was present in its undivided wholeness. That, at least, is how apologists like Justin Martyr (100?–165?) made their defense of Christianity. In the eighteenth century, however, the old question of Christianity and other religions was asked again out of quite different presuppositions.

The English deists, for instance, did not start from the conviction that Christianity possessed a unique and superior revelation setting it apart from other religions. On the contrary, their initial assumption was that where the Christian faith differed from other religious faiths it could not possibly be affirming anything true or essential. Against the traditional claim that God had given a unique and exclusive revelation in Jesus Christ, without which salvation was not possible, the deists argued that there had to be a common religion of humanity and that Christianity could claim to be true only insofar as it embodied the common religion. Everything peculiar to Christianity was to be discarded as merely accidental; only the universal elements that appeared in all religions, Christianity among them, could be accepted as truth.

Modern historians of religions may smile at this bold conviction that if you only look hard enough you will uncover the common denominator in all humanity's religions; these days many of them will say that it is not even possible to frame a working definition of "religion" to cover all the possible instances of the class. There was something naive, no doubt, about the deistic theory of religion. And the results may strike one as a little threadbare: the minimal "religion of reason," as they called it, amounted to little more than the beliefs that there is a God, that God rewards virtue, and that therefore a person's ultimate destiny hangs upon leading a virtuous life. But if that sounds like pretty thin stuff, bear in mind that the deists had posed an urgent question and answered it with a radicalness which plunged the churches into bitter controversy. For what, if anything, had they left for Christians to believe about Christ? Was he just one among many teachers of the good life?

Finally, there is the further question: What do we actually *know* about Christ? The eighteenth century saw the beginnings of historical criticism of the Bible. Traditionally, Christians had set the Bible apart from other documents of the ancient world: it was not to be read like other literature, as you might read Herodotus, or Livy, or Tacitus. It contained the verbally inspired oracles of God from cover to cover, and Christians did not doubt that as they read the four Gospels they were reading actual events of history, reliably reported under the moving of the Spirit. The contrast with the new, eighteenth-century approach is clearly signaled in the title of a work by G. E. Lessing (1729–81): *New Hypothesis Concerning the Evangelists Regarded as Purely Human Historians* (1778). And the most extreme results of the new approach can be seen in the theory of H. S. Reimarus (1694–1768), in the *Wolfenbüttel Fragments*, that the real historical Jesus was a misguided Jewish prophet, whose career ended in tragedy and despair: Jesus foretold the coming of the kingdom of God, and he was wrong.

Any theologian who is to face up to all these questions has a formidable agenda. But that is exactly the way it has been for the Christian theologian ever since the eighteenth century. The problem is not only the practical one of conveying faith in Christ in language that can be preached in the pulpit as well as learned in seminaries. Luther knew all about *that* problem. For the present-day ministers of the Word, there is the added difficulty of preaching Christ responsibly—in a way that tackles modern questions of which, for the most part, Luther never dreamed. And this was the task Schleiermacher undertook to investigate as the pioneer of modern theology.

RELIGION FIRST, THEN CHRISTIANITY?

Schleiermacher acknowledged that a credibility gap had opened between the dogmas of the church and the outlook of the Enlightenment, and he took with complete earnestness the three intellectual difficulties I have listed. But he went about his task in a spirit totally different from that of the Enlightenment philosophers. Reimarus, for instance, held that the only way in which we can arrive at a genuine understanding of Jesus is by making the effort to forget all that the church has taught us about the incarnation and the Trinity, dogmas which in his opinion had their source not in the Jesus of history but in deliberate lies fabricated by his disillusioned disciples. For Schleiermacher, by contrast, the dogmatic task was not merely to set the dogmas aside but to understand and improve them.

In other words, Schleiermacher took his bearings strictly from the standpoint of the church's faith, which he defined as certainty of the redeeming influence of Christ. The christological problem, therefore, is to understand the Christ of faith: to get back to the faith that gave birth to the dogma. But this means that Christians must ask *themselves*, What is it that we in fact owe to Jesus? and, What does this say about his person? In Schleiermacher's own terms, they are to attribute to the Redeemer the "dignity" that his "activity" demands. Undoubtedly, it was his own profound and indelible sense of indebtedness to the Redeemer that enabled him to pose the question in this fashion. If he succeeded, as I for one believe, in renewing Christian theology at the end of the Age of Reason, then the explanation for his success is certainly the one given by Alexander Schweizer (1808–88), perhaps his most faithful disciple: Schleiermacher restored the confidence of the Christian consciousness in its own content. After the Enlightenment, the Age of Reason, that was no small achievement.

But it did not happen all at once. And I want to distinguish, as briefly and clearly as I can, between the first christological efforts of the *Speeches on Religion*, the crucial shift in *The Celebration of Christmas*, and the mature standpoint of *The Christian Faith*. The speeches constituted the revolutionary manifesto from which the birth of the new era in theology is commonly dated, and *The Christian Faith* was the culmination of Schleiermacher's theological labors. Between them stands the modest little Christmas dialogue; for our purposes, it has a significance way beyond its unassuming size and style.

On Religion: Speeches to its Cultured Despisers was addressed to those modern men and women whose education has interested them in just about everything except religion. They have created for themselves a rich, exciting, and rewarding earthly life, and they no longer stand in need of eternity. Schleiermacher's astute defense of religion argues that in actual fact to be religious is also a necessary part of what it means to be human; and the human spirit, in which the cultured despisers so rightly rejoice, is sadly impoverished if the religious side of it is denied, ignored, or suppressed. Rightly understood, religion is the inspiration of science, of art, of morality, and of everything else the despisers claim to cherish. Are they, then, willing to settle for a truncated humanity? Or will they look again and recognize that true religion is not just the dogmas and usages they despise but a "sense of the infinite," which every soul that looks can find within? Nothing is more effective in freeing the choked-up springs of religion, Schleiermacher suggests, than the cultivation of art and the imagination. But the artistic sense is one of the things the cultivated despisers cherish most. "See, then," he concludes, "whether you wish it or not, the goal of your highest present efforts is also the resurrection of religion. . . . I celebrate you as, however unintentionally, the rescuers and guardians of religion."

Only in the last speech does Schleiermacher try to carry his readers the second mile, that is, to persuade them that the religion they need is Christianity. I think it is fair to say that he immediately finds himself in difficulties. True, he quickly disposes of the "religion of reason" so dear to the English deists; it is, he holds, a mere armchair construct, "a vague, shabby, indigent idea that as such can never actually exist." And he insists that you have to settle *somewhere* if you are to have a residence at all in the world of religion. But why in Christianity? Schleiermacher has so set up the terms of the discussion that he can present Christianity only as one option among many—one of the infinite variety of forms that the spirit of religion freely assumes. "Nothing is more unchristian," he admits, "than to seek uniformity in religion." Of course, he does his best to commend Christianity. Jesus, he says, is indeed "the lofty author of the most splendid there has so far been in religion." Still, Jesus never claimed to be the only mediator. And to say that he is the best so far leaves open the possibility of better things to come. Christianity, Schleiermacher confidently asserts, will still have a long history. But if the time should arrive when there would be so little corruption that humanity made only calm and steady progress, then his solemn promise is this: "I would gladly stand on the ruins of the religion I honor." Truly a remarkable confession, coming as it does from a Christian apologist!

Well, perhaps Schleiermacher was so perfectly confident
about the future of Christianity that he thought he could make
the promise without any risk. The argument of the *Speeches on
Religion* is admittedly subtle, and I do not want to leave the impression that we can quickly dispose of it. Schleiermacher made
interpretation of his original text even harder by introducing
changes in subsequent editions. In the second edition (1806), for
instance, he inserted a phrase that seems to run counter to the
main drift of his arguments. He first said that anyone is a Christian whose religion centers on the same fundamental idea as
Christ's religion did, that is, the idea of mediation, however he
or she came by it. He then added in the second edition that such
a person, when shown Christ, "will also be bound to acknowledge him as the one who has become historically the center of
all mediation." The insertion posed difficulties of its own, so in
the third edition (1821) Schleiermacher found it necessary to
add a further explanation of the addition. But for now I must
set the details aside and be content to make just one observa-
tion: Schleiermacher tries in the *Speeches on Religion* to commend religion first, then Christianity, and I think the result is
that he has great difficulty doing Christianity justice. His first
attempt to show the significance of Christ falls far short of
traditional Christian sentiments. And that is where the
Christmas dialogue comes in.

THE ATTRACTION OF CHRIST

The dialogue marks an apparent shift in Schleiermacher's
method, or at least in his strategy. The Christian consciousness,
he now decides, is where reflection about Jesus Christ must actually begin. I have already mentioned the conviction that lies
behind this shift: the proper context for theological argument is
the living piety of the Christian community, because reflection
and argument are strictly secondary to a more fundamental and
intuitive relationship with the things of the Spirit. Hence the
high-powered argument of the men is carefully preceded by

those fascinating, if sometimes quaint, remarks about the virtues of music, childhood, and the feminine character. And the dialogue is brought to a close when the pietist Joseph interrupts the argument and insists on leading the company back to the piano.

In a sense, this is simply an extension of the distinction, made already in the *Speeches on Religion*, between life and doctrine, piety and thought. But now the distinction is invoked in order to set *Christology* on a fresh footing, and it enables Schleiermacher to face as well another of our three difficulties: doubt concerning the reliability of the Gospel records.

One of the characters in the dialogue is an amiable but skeptical lawyer named Leonard. Mischievously, he accepts the challenge to make a speech in praise of Christmas, and he proposes that the real wonder of the Christmas festival is that it induces us to believe things about Jesus which a serious historian could only consider unlikely or absurd. The Gospel narratives yield nothing but conflicting views of Jesus; the marvel of Christmas is that the celebrations nonetheless make us believers, who happily believe the unbelievable.

With gentle irony Leonard has posed the question of the historical Jesus: modern historical scholarship seems to have removed Jesus beyond all possibility of historical knowledge, and he has disappeared in a crowd of squabbling New Testament scholars. Schleiermacher now makes his crucial move: he does not have his other characters, Ernest and Edward, reply to Leonard on historical grounds but strictly on the grounds of the Christian experience of redemption. We begin from the Christmas joy shared among Christian people, and we ask, What must be its source? The present power of the new life leads us back to the person of the Redeemer as its only possible point of origin.

So the stage is set for the definitive statement of Schleiermacher's Christology in *The Christian Faith*. Taking his stand within the believing community, he begins unequivocally with the Christ of faith and asks, What is it that, as a matter of fact, he does for those who believe in him and belong to his fellowship? Schleiermacher thinks that if Christians search their actual experience of the Redeemer, his activity will be seen to resemble the attractive power of a strong personality. What is received in the preaching of the Word today is in substance no different from what the first disciples received in their calling by the earthly Christ, only now the impression and the influence of his personality come less directly through the biblical *picture* of him set forth in the church's proclamation.

And yet, to the consciousness of someone in the grip of conversion, all human mediation vanishes and Christ is immediately present in all his redeeming and reconciling activity—prophetic, priestly, and kingly. Nor, as Schleiermacher sees it, is this sense of immediacy an illusion: the power of Christ himself is in the communication of the Word, insofar as it continues Christ's Word. The only difference is that Christ's presentation of himself is now mediated by those who proclaim him; but since they are his instruments, the activity originates from him and is essentially his. Even his original influence— though purely spiritual in that it was exercised over the hearts of men and women—was "mediated" in the sense that it was exercised through his bodily appearance. His present influence does not therefore become merely derivative and indirect simply because today it comes through the written Word's picture of his nature and activity.

But what is the secret of his attraction? Schleiermacher finds it in the unique strength of Christ's sense of God. Once again, it is a matter of rightly analyzing Christian experience: we must then see that Christ redeems by drawing men and women into the power of his own awareness of God. And again Schleiermacher is convinced that this is just how it happened when Christ called his disciples. For his message had the character of a "self-proclamation": his words gave expression to his own sense of unique relationship with his Father, and in this lay the power of his influence.

Schleiermacher developed this line of thought in his lectures on the life of Jesus (1832), which had the distinction of being the first course of academic lectures ever given on the subject. There he traced Jesus' story as the growing awareness of a special relationship with God—from the first recognition that he must be about his Father's business to his final triumph over the cross. But we must set the details aside and hold on firmly to the central point: the Christ of faith works on believers through the power of his "God-consciousness." Schleiermacher suggested in the *Life of Jesus* that we might think of God-consciousness as a kind of scale. At the bottom are those who never have a thought about God that is not suggested to them from the outside, or who even perhaps resist the emergence of any such thought. But it must be possible to conceive of someone at the top of the scale in whose life every significant moment is permeated by awareness of God. And in *The Christian Faith* this is how Schleiermacher thinks of Christ and how he accounts for Christ's unique power over the lives of Christians. Whatever historical difficulties there may be in the New Testament, Schleiermacher was convinced that precisely this maximal God-consciousness shines through the Gospel narratives. Here, then, is the dignity that Christ's activity attests.

For myself, I must admit that I think there are some weak points in Schleiermacher's argument. But I have been fully persuaded that the fundamental move he made opened up a new and positive stage in christological thinking. He began neither with ancient dogmas nor with ancient history, but with what every Christian experiences, and he sought to give an honest account of it that would not run away from the intellectual problems of the modern world. "Quite simply," he assured Lücke, "I have interrogated the feeling common to all devout Christians, and I have only tried to describe it." It is easy to see why

Schleiermacher placed on the title page of *The Christian Faith* a motto from Anselm: "He who has not experienced will not understand."

Is he right? Is it the case that if Christians look into themselves, what they find is an influence of Jesus that is at once similar to the experience they have of strong personalities and yet unique in coming from a sense of God to which they know no parallel? Is this, further, a sufficient point of departure for a theological estimate of Christ's person? And how well has Schleiermacher answered the three intellectual difficulties posed for Christology by the Age of Reason?

The questions remain. But at least his strategy and its possibilities are now clear. By pegging everything on the Redeemer's unique consciousness of God, Schleiermacher was able to claim, first, that Christ was not just one teacher of the common religion of humanity; second, that the Gospel story does not need to be infallible in all details if only it verifies and mediates the picture of him; and, third, that there is no need to conceive of God's presence in Christ as a conjunction of two natures. "For," says Schleiermacher, "to ascribe to Christ an absolutely powerful consciousness of God and to attribute to him an existence of God in him are entirely one and the same thing."

3. The Acts of God

There are many people who not only profess themselves opposed to any belief in God but suppose they really are, while actually they are only rebelling against the conventional presentations of it and have by no means banished from themselves all the spiritual affections that rest on consciousness of God.

The strictest dogmaticians have always acknowledged that the divine preservation, as the absolute dependence of all events and changes on God, and natural causation, as the total determination of everything that happens by the universal nexus, are neither separated from each other nor limited by each other, but are the same thing—only seen from different viewpoints.

Schleiermacher, *The Christian Faith*

A former next-door neighbor of mine was an avid football fan who liked to follow the "Irish"; if I remember rightly, he was a Notre Dame alumnus. But in the Chicago suburbs it is not usually possible to pick up the away games live on television from South Bend. He solved the problem one summer when I was on vacation: I came back to find an enormous antenna towering over my two-story home. I should think it must have been capable of picking up any Big Ten game, not only from South Bend but within several hundred miles. It was like living next door to the headquarters of the state police; only the flashing red light that warns off friendly aircraft was missing.

Seeing I was a bit apprehensive, my neighbor pointed out all the fine features of his new antenna. It was sunk deep in concrete, and he demonstrated the sturdiness of the metal frame by climbing up it for me. This, I grant, was impressive, because he had a footballer's physique that had spread with advancing years. So, I was not particularly anxious when he moved and left the antenna standing.

But it fell. During a windstorm the antenna fell on the front of my house, buckling the gutters, and then crashed through my favorite evergreen onto the lawn. Now my lawn is not a suburban showpiece, I must admit, and one of my new neighbors pointed out that the antenna could have fallen on one of my children. "Somebody up there," she said, "is watching over us." But, not having quite regained my composure, I replied thoughtlessly, "Then why didn't he stop it from falling on my gutters?"

The insurance agent was theologically of the same persuasion as my neighbor: what had happened, he explained, was an act of God, and therefore his company could not accept financial responsibility. But when a repairman came, he attributed the fall to metal deterioration plus the force of the wind; he did not mention God. Presumably, neither my neighbors nor the insurance agent would have cared to deny the repairman's diagnosis. They would not have said he was a wicked skeptic who disbelieved in God. And I found myself asking, What exactly *did* God do? What does he *ever* do? What do we mean by "acts of God"?

THE SENSE OF GOD

What has this to do with Schleiermacher? The answer is that there is plainly something missing in what I have said of him so far, and the story of my neighbor's antenna makes the omission only too clear. I have tried to show how a theological program emerged from Schleiermacher's intellectual and religious odyssey and how he put the program to work on the problem of Christology. He was convinced that many of the formulas by which the church conveyed its faith in Christ had outlived their usefulness. There was not merely a communication gap, which robbed them of their practical utility for nurturing a living faith in Christ; there was also a credibility gap opened up by "enlightened" intellectuals, who thought the two-natures doctrine logically confused, could see in Jesus no more than one among many teachers of a universal religion, and denied that a purely historical study of the Gospels could possibly discover in them the church's Christ.

Schleiermacher's attempted solution was to get back behind the church's formulas to actual Christian experience, and so to see whether better formulas could be devised which would preserve the intention of the old ones without their defects. We need only to interrogate the Christian consciousness of every believer, so he argued, to reach the conclusion that in actual fact the Christ of faith works today, as he did in the days of his flesh, through the power of his unique God-consciousness. It is this unique God-consciousness that enables us to affirm the presence of God in Christ without the two-natures doctrine, to distinguish the man Jesus from other men, and to affirm the sufficiency of the New Testament documents even if they give neither a full biography of Jesus nor the credal formulas of the ancient church.

But what does it mean to talk about a "consciousness of God"? Plainly, something decisive is missing: there remains an immense hiatus in the proposed christological revision until it is determined that the expression "consciousness of God" has a specifiable meaning. And I must now come back to the qualification I said I would have to add to Strauss's remark that Schleiermacher's dogmatics really has but one dogma. It is certainly true that Schleiermacher tries to relate everything (as he puts it) to the redemption effected by Jesus of Nazareth, but it does not follow that everything in his theology is deduced from a single center. Richard R. Niebuhr suggests that Schleiermacher's theology is not "Christo-centric" but "Christomorphic." Christology, in other words, is not the absolute center of the system, but the system as a whole is shaped or formed by Christology.

Schleiermacher held, in fact, that in the life of the Christian *two* elements are always and inseparably present: a general awareness of God and a special relation to Christ. What the revelation of God in Christ does is to determine in a special way the awareness of God that is a universal and invariable ingredient in all human consciousness and appears most purely in the monotheistic religions. The general awareness of God constitutes what Schleiermacher called an "original revelation"; it is distinct from the special or historical revelation in Christ but in Christian experience cannot be separated from it. It is this common human consciousness that he called, not very happily perhaps, "pious feeling," and he described it to Lücke as "the original utterance of an immediate existential relationship," that is, the expression of a way of being in relation to reality that lies at a deeper level than thought or action. He was confident that this relationship belongs to human nature as such; all it takes to recognize it, he said, is a little introspection.

So, then, although it is the revelation in Christ that determines the Christian understanding of God, to answer the question, What does it mean to be conscious of God at all? is within the capability of anyone, Christian or not, who has learned the art of looking into his or her own consciousness. Now this will surely strike anyone who knows the intellectual history of the Age of Reason as a remarkably daring claim. How could one possibly say by the end of the eighteenth century that a sense of God is always and invariably present in human consciousness, so that every event that happens must somehow be thought of as filled with the presence of God or, in common religious parlance, as an "act of God"?

THE RETREAT OF GOD

The truth seems to be that by the end of the eighteenth century God had become a hypothesis of which there was no more need. What was there left for God to do? The change in scientific habits of thought struck a serious blow at religious ways of viewing the world. It would be oversimplifying history if we said that the story begins with a God who does everything, moves on to a God who acts occasionally, and ends with a superannuated

God who need not exist at all. But that is not so very far from
the truth. We can in any case look at these three variants simply
as logical alternatives, not worrying overmuch whether they
belong in a single historical sequence.

Anyone examining the writings of the seventeenth-century
Puritans will find them speaking as though God and the Devil
were engaged in a constant struggle to possess their souls. That
is certainly the way John Bunyan (1628–88) writes in his classic
Grace Abounding to the Chief of Sinners (1666). God is always
putting thoughts into Bunyan's mind, ordering his ways, directing him to predetermined ends. In Puritan piety, God is not just
up there "watching," to use the phrase of my neighbor, but actually controlling the entire course of events, doing whatever
gets done. In short, God does *everything*; God has even the
Devil on a short leash.

I like to illustrate this notion of the God who does all with
a pleasant story I first came across in William James's
(1842–1910) *The Varieties of Religious Experience*. It concerns
Robert Lyde, an otherwise forgotten English sailor who in 1689
was taken captive aboard a French ship along with a young lad.
The two of them, according to Lyde's *A True and Exact
Account* (1693), attacked the crew of seven Frenchmen, killed
two, and made the other five prisoners; and so they brought the
enemy ship home to England. Here is Lyde's description of this
remarkable feat of supernatural strength; I give it in the "slightly abridged" version in James's book, except that I have taken
the liberty of abridging it a little further.

> With the assistance of God I kept my feet when they three and
> one more did strive to throw me down. . . . Then I looked about
> for a marlin spike or anything else to strike them withal. But see-
> ing nothing, I said, "Lord! what shall I do?" Then casting up
> my eye upon my left side, and seeing a marlin spike hanging, I
> jerked my right arm and took hold, and struck the point four
> times about a quarter of an inch deep into the skull of that man
> that had hold of my left arm. . . . [One of his captors then

hauled the marlin spike away from him.] But through God's
wonderful providence! it either fell out of his hand, or else he
threw it down, and at this time the Almighty God gave me
strength enough to take one man in one hand, and throw at the
other's head: and looking about again to see anything to strike
them withal, but seeing nothing, I said, "Lord! what shall I do
now?" And then it pleased God to put me in mind of my knife in
my pocket. And although two of the men had hold of my right
arm, yet God Almighty strengthened me so that I put my right
hand into my right pocket, drew out the knife and
sheath . . . and then cut the man's throat with it that had his
back to my breast: and he immediately dropt down, and scarce
ever stirred after.

A fascinating narrative! But somehow it does not sound right.
That is not the way most people these days tell a story. Among
the varieties of religious experience, James classifies it as ex-
pressing a "more primitive style of religious thought." But what
is primitive about it? Why is it that the account strikes us modern men and women as wrongheaded and even amusing? Is it
because Lyde's God so plainly favors the English? Or is it
perhaps because his God helps him do some very nasty things,
like driving a marlin spike into one Frenchman's skull and slit-
ting another one's throat with a pocketknife? Well, I'm sure
that is all part of it. But the heart of the matter, I think, lies
elsewhere. It seems to me that the reason why we tend to adopt a
critical, or at least a distant, stance toward this kind of narrative is that the references to what God did strike us as redun-
dant. They really are not needed to tell us what happened; they
add nothing to the facts. A report in the *New York Times* the
next morning ("All the news that's fit to print") would not say
that God was pleased to put Lyde in mind of the pocketknife; it
would say, more simply, Lyde remembered his knife.

Maybe the unadorned, matter-of-fact way of speaking was
how less-primitive men and women had come to express
themselves long before the rise of modern science. But by the
end of the seventeenth century, there was an added inducement

for dropping the devout, all-inclusive providence-talk of Robert
Lyde. In 1687 Sir Isaac Newton (1642–1727) published his *Principia Mathematica*, that unparalleled symbol of a new attitude
toward nature; it marked the culmination of a century-old attempt to reduce the events of nature to regular laws. In itself,
the notion of an orderly nature posed no difficulties for the
sophisticated theologians of Newton's day; they were already
inclined to a rigidly deterministic view of providence and
predestination, and they could simply identify the orderly
progress of nature as the outworking of God's decrees. The laws
of nature were the laws of God. But in the long run the idea of
natural law did prove to be problematic for religious faith.

The image that began to dominate the scientific imagination
was that of the cosmic machine, which, once it had been put
together and set going by the divine artificer, continued to run
on its own. A watch when wound does not need further attention if its design is flawless. The busy, active, engaged God of
the Puritans withdrew from the scene of natural occurrences
and human affairs; God came to be admired as its one-time
Maker, but only in very rare circumstances was God called upon
to modify the course of events, to make something turn out differently than it otherwise might, or perhaps just to account for
something that continued to resist scientific explanation. Instead of a continually active God, we then have a God who does
not everything but *something*. "Acts of God" are strictly occasional events. And if we take with a grain of salt the insurance
agent's explanation that the fall of my antenna was wholly an
act of God, is the alternative to divide the responsibility and to
say that God did not make the antenna fall, but God did prevent
it from falling on a child?

I suspect that what we have here in the "something" view of
divine providence comes close to normal modern piety, that is, a
religious view of things that has been reduced severely by our
changed habits of thought about nature. It apparently makes
more sense to us than the "everything" view, which seems to

credit (or reproach) God with too much. But the reduced view, too, has its obvious difficulty, as the progress of scientific thought made painfully clear. How do you stop "something" from becoming "nothing"?

Why, in other words, is metal fatigue and a sudden gust of high wind not a full, complete, and sufficient explanation of the falling antenna? It seems one is driven to the consistently deistic view that the Creator, having fashioned the world, has no further business with it but dwells in eternal Sabbath rest. Of course, a religion of sorts is perfectly compatible with such a notion of the deity, especially if it is maintained that the Creator imparted to the world an essentially moral character, establishing its moral as well as its natural laws. But the final act of exclusion comes in the skepticism that asks whether the God who does nothing is needed anymore, or ever was.

Perhaps God never did do anything but is in fact a product of the human imagination, which finds it hard to picture order without an orderer, or design without a designer. So David Hume (1711-76), for instance, the great Scottish unbeliever, did not doubt that the world makes on the human mind a strong impression of artifice, but suggested in his *Dialogues Concerning Natural Religion* (1779) that it was only a matter of "habit, caprice, or inclination" whether or not one compared the cause of nature to a mind, that is, an artificer. As far as Hume could see, nothing important hung upon the choice between the skeptic and the dogmatist, although he did firmly believe that popular talk about God was liable to issue in superstition and a diseased preoccupation with one's own soul. In other words, belief in the Artificer God makes no difference to our knowledge of the way the world goes, but in its popular varieties it does make a regrettable difference to the way we behave.

How, then, could Schleiermacher possibly assert that an awareness of God is a universal and invariable ingredient in every person's consciousness? The progress of scientific and philosophical thought in the seventeenth and eighteenth centuries seems to force on us the conclusion that belief in God is entirely optional, and that it makes precious little difference whether or not one has it.

GOD AS THE LIFE WITHIN

Undaunted apologists in England still tried after Hume to refurbish the old theistic proofs. It is one of the oddities of intellectual history that the classic English work on natural theology, the *Natural Theology* (1802) of William Paley (1743–1805), was published more than twenty years after Hume's *Dialogues*. To the skeptic's doubts about whether there is an Artificer God, the English apologist in effect replied: "Oh, yes there is!" It cannot be said, even by a judgment of charity, that Paley really confronted Hume's arguments.

In Schleiermacher's Germany the situation was quite different. Two fierce public controversies, the pantheism and atheism controversies, made it doubtful whether religion's best interests were really tied to the notion of the divine watchmaker. As Goethe asked, "What kind of God were he who only pushed from outside?" Many of the German intellectuals turned away from the "extramundane God," as they called the deity outside, and found their inspiration in the view of Benedict Spinoza (1632–77) that God and nature must be reconceived as together constituting an indivisible unity. Surprisingly perhaps, they could thus be said to have agreed, in effect, with the skeptic Philo in Hume's *Dialogues*, who is made to say: "It were better, therefore, never to look beyond the present material world. By supposing it to contain the principle of its order within itself, we really assert it to be God; and the sooner we arrive at that divine Being so much the better."

As a Christian theologian, Schleiermacher could not permit an identification of God and nature such as Philo's remark implies. He knew perfectly well that one no longer has the Christian God either if one says with deism that some events fall outside the divine activity, or if one says with pantheism, as

commonly understood, that talk of divine activity adds nothing
to talk of natural events. But if we think of Christian theism as
moving between these polar opposites, it is plain that he agreed
with the shift made by some of the most eminent German
thinkers *toward* the pantheistic pole. Hence, it cannot be said
that his idea of God was entirely original; it put him in the
mainstream of German thought at the turn of the century. Still,
his approach to the problem of God was characteristically his
own.

Schleiermacher tried to set the dogma of Christ on a new
footing by first moving back behind doctrinal formulas to living
experience. He did the same in trying to set the concept of God
also on a new footing, only here the experience in question was
not peculiarly Christian but universally human. He asked, What
is it in common human experience that generates talk about
God? and, How is this talk of God connected with all the other
ways in which we speak about the world around us? This approach to the problem of "God-talk" is among the most permanently fruitful items in Schleiermacher's theological legacy.
With or without acknowledgments to him, many present-day
theologians begin their entire enterprise by attempting to show
the necessity for God-talk and its anchorage in common human
experience.

Unfortunately, Schleiermacher's analysis of human consciousness and its necessarily religious character, however fruitful, is also among the most difficult and hotly debated items in
his legacy. I shall have to take the risk of a few shortcuts. Indeed, I want to be so bold as to focus on one shift that he, like
others in Germany, proposed in our ways of thinking and
speaking of God. This requires me to catch his argument in the
middle rather than at the beginning, that is, when he has already
moved on from the elemental God-consciousness—the "feeling
of absolute dependence"—to the ways in which it is modified
by our experience of the natural and social environments. While
it is true that this will not permit me to do full justice to his argu-

ment *for* the necessity of God-consciousness, it will, however, establish that the proposed shift takes the sting out of an allegedly scientific argument *against* belief in God. It is somewhat the same shift that we find closer to our own day in Paul Tillich's (1886–1965) familiar definition of God as "the ground of being." As a matter of fact, Schleiermacher himself already used "ground-language" in his statements about the highest being.

Perhaps, at the risk of oversimplification, I can make my point provisionally in my own way before looking more closely at his. It seems to me that the heart of the matter is a shift in the dominant *image* of God. Think for a moment of that splendid passage in which Isaiah asks the question, "To whom then will you liken God, or what likeness compare with him?" (Isa. 40: 18). The prophet tells us it is a mockery to compare God to an idol fashioned by a craftsman's hand. For

> It is he who sits above the circle of the earth,
>   and its inhabitants are like grasshoppers;
> who stretches out the heavens like a curtain,
>   and spreads them like a tent to dwell in;
> who brings princes to nought,
>   and makes the rulers of the earth as nothing.
>   (vv. 22–23)

Now think next of another marvelous sample of religious poetry, the hymn "Immortal, Invisible, God Only Wise" by Walter Chalmers Smith (1824–1908). The third verse goes like this:

> To all, life Thou givest—to both great and small;
>   In all life Thou livest, the true life of all;
> We blossom and flourish as leaves on the tree,
>   And wither and perish—but naught changeth Thee.

Plainly, there is a contrast between two images of God in these two poetic utterances: the contrast between the "Man Upstairs" (to use one of our own slightly irreverent colloquialisms) and the "life within." They are not, of course, the only images of God in Christian literature, and it is not a question of which is the right one. Each of them gives expression to some aspect of Christian experience of God, and each may therefore have its appropriate context. Schleiermacher's point, in essence, is that we will make more progress in dealing with the problem of God and science if we move in *that* context to the image of God as the life within, or something like it, for the discussion of the problem is often confused by false analogies between divine activity and the personal acts of individuals. In one place in *The Christian Faith*, Schleiermacher suggests it would be better if we thought of God's relation to us not as the relation of one self to other selves but as like the relation my own self has to my mental activities.

Schleiermacher gave his first reflections on God in the *Speeches on Religion*. There he argued that to be religious is to sense the unity of all finite things, including oneself, with the infinite, so that the most basic definition identifies God as "the highest unity." And he broad-mindedly suggested that it did not matter much whether the religious person pictured this underlying unity of things as a personal spirit or not, although he thought that most religious persons inevitably would do so. But if he proposed this standpoint as irenic—a happy tolerance of different concepts of God—he must have been surprised by the public reaction.

In particular, his own ecclesiastical superior, a man named F. S. G. Sack (1738–1817), wrote him an angry letter of rebuke in which he accused him of selling out to pantheism but hiding his true convictions under the cloak of duplicity. If he continued to preach in the customary language about the bonds of thankfulness, obedience, and trust that relate us to the highest being, he could do so only as a man who believed none of it in his heart, but to avoid giving offense used a manner of speech that had either no meaning at all for him or else a wholly unconventional meaning.

Schleiermacher's gentle reply is crucial to a fair understanding. Unfortunately, right down to the present day one will find it said of him, without qualification, that he wanted to eliminate anthropomorphism, that is, speaking as though God were the "Somebody Up There." In actual fact, he admitted to Sack, without *some* anthropomorphism nothing in religion could ever be put into words. It is the dominant way of speaking about God in Scripture, including the discourses of Jesus, and in Christianity generally. But it does not follow that without further ado God may therefore be formally assigned the attribute of personality. In other words, Christians do not really want to say that God is a person exactly like them; they admit they have to give some qualifications.

To make his position clearer, Schleiermacher added an "explanation" in the third edition (1821) of the *Speeches on Religion.* He has been accused, he writes, of preferring the impersonal form of thinking about God, and this is even being spoken of as his atheism or pantheism ("Spinozism"). In actual fact, he had supposed that the Christian thing to do was to acknowledge piety in all its forms, including the personal form. There is a virtual necessity at the highest stage of piety to appropriate the idea of God as person, whenever the heart enters into immediate converse with the highest being; problems arise only when the limitations in the idea of personality are not recognized. The most profound of the church fathers, Schleiermacher points out, have always been careful; indeed, if one were to assemble all their qualifications of divine personality, one could as easily say that they denied personality to God as that they ascribed it to him. And on the whole it would be better if we spoke of God as the living God rather than the personal God, because "living God" suffices to make the essential point: the underlying unity of things is not material or blindly mechanical.

GOD AND NATURE'S LAWS

The significance of this invitation to shift our theological concept of God, if not the medium of our daily converse with God, is brought out with powerful effect in *The Christian Faith*. Schleiermacher admits that for many devout persons the religious consciousness is most in evidence when something appears to interrupt the regular course of events. In other words, God is popularly thought of as active when intervening in human affairs. But this will not do theologically for two reasons. First, it forgets the limits of the idea of personality and reduces God to the measure of, as we are putting it, the Somebody Up There, who acts as a person among persons. God is then drawn into the domain of finite causes and so is himself made finite. As Schleiermacher sees it, God to be God must be understood as doing everything, not as simply watching for occasions to act sometimes. God's omnipotence does and causes everything.

Second, the notion of an intervening deity would totally abrogate the scientific concept of nature, according to which nature proceeds on a strictly regular, uninterrupted, law-governed course. And it would be disastrous if devout believers should imagine they had a vested interest in resisting scientific explanation. "As our knowledge of the world became complete," Schleiermacher points out, "the development of the pious consciousness in ordinary life would completely cease."

What, then, is the alternative if we are still to speak about God, indeed, about a God who in some sense does everything? Schleiermacher's answer was, as one could easily anticipate, that we must learn to think of the law-governed course of nature not as being blindly mechanical but as being pervaded by the presence of the living God. The world as such has meaning and purpose; it does not acquire religious significance by virtue of periodic divine incursions. At the bottom of things, Schleiermacher found a creative impulse—a "divine decree" as he called it in the old language—that directs nature and history to a specific end. He identified this end as the raising of humanity to a higher level of consciousness, which, simply put, is "personhood."

Against the inadequacies of popular piety, therefore, we must hold that consciousness of God rises in exact proportion to our ability to think of ourselves as placed in a closed system of nature in which the regular course of events is never interrupted. God is the living God who preserves the system, directing it uninterruptedly toward certain ends. It cannot be religious to think of God as intervening in the world, for this could only mean that, for a fleeting moment at least, the world had slipped out of God's control and taken an unintended course. In Schleiermacher's view, nothing could be more utterly destructive of devout trust in the meaning and purpose of the world, or in the omnipotence and love of its underlying cause—the living God. To be religious, then, according to Schleiermacher—or, what is the same thing, to be conscious of God—is to trust in the goodness of the order that science investigates. It has nothing to do with searching for gaps in the scientific world picture. There is no room for conflict between science and religion.

There will always be devout Christians for whom such a solution to the problem of science and religion can only appear as a betrayal of religion; for them, the profit of godliness lies in the power of prayer to obtain divine intervention in a train of events that would otherwise turn out differently. Schleiermacher was fully aware of this, and one of his most interesting and powerful sermons addressed the problem directly. If at least one test of theology is made in the pulpit, then I know of no better way to wind up our entire discussion than by referring to the sermon, remarkable testimony that it is to Schleiermacher's own personal faith and his pastoral care for the faith of others.

Entitled "The Power of Prayer in Relation to Outward Circumstances," it takes as its text Christ's agony in the Garden of Gethsemane (Matt. 26:36–46). Is it right for us to seek the fulfillment of our wishes in prayer? Schleiermacher knows the risks: petition may lead either to disappointment and uncertainty, or else, if the request is granted, to the presumption that one must be the special object of God's pleasure. Still, his answer is that children may of course tell their Father what it is

that they desire; Christ himself in the garden laid his wishes
before his Heavenly Father. But there, in the experience of
Christ, lies an important lesson: what Christ wanted was not
granted him. The purpose of prayer, Schleiermacher infers, is
not to bend God's will to our wishes but to bend our wishes to
God's will. Christ's object in Gethsemane was to reconcile himself to the will of his Father; he prayed until his anxiety and
dread were gone. From the pattern of Christ's own example,
then, Schleiermacher formulates a general rule of prayer: God is
always to be approached as the Unchangeable One,

> in whose mind no new thought and no new decision can arise
> since he said to himself, "All that I have made is good." . . . If,
> because of the way he has ordained the tissue of events, you
> must do without what you wish for, you have your compensa-
> tion in all the goodness that you see in the world. . . . But the
> Wise One is also kind. He will not let you suffer and do without
> solely for the sake of others. His will is that for the justified man
> everything should work together for his own good. So arises
> trust that, within the whole, notice has been taken of us, too,
> however small a part we may be.

To be religious and to pray, Schleiermacher says, are one and
the same thing. But the prayer without ceasing that the apostle
commends (1 Thess. 5:17) consists, he thinks, in the art of com-
bining every important thought we have with thought about
God: a thought of the Creator when our eye rests on God's
works, a glad sense of God's love when we are enjoying God's
gifts, a thankful sense of God's support when we succeed in
some good work, and so on. Schleiermacher does not doubt the
efficacy of such prayer: it has the power to keep us from sin. It
does not change the will of God, but he saw that it does change
those who pray, transforming their wishes into humble acceptance. Prayer, in this sense, is identical with the religion, or
piety, or God-consciousness of which Schleiermacher wrote in
The Christian Faith. To be conscious of God is not to invite
divine intervention in the world but to acknowledge that the

course of the world is sustained by omnipotent love and is therefore good.

CHRIST AND THE SENSE OF GOD

What does it mean to be "conscious of God"? We now have, in barest outline, Schleiermacher's answer. What does it tell us about the notion of an "act of God"? We are obliged to conclude that strictly speaking, or at the level of dogmatic correctness, acts of God have no place in Schleiermacher's thought. To talk of God's *acts* (in the plural) is to relapse into anthropomorphism or, as we would say, mythology: it is to imagine God as one personal agent among others in space and time, making ad hoc decisions, doing this and doing that as the occasion demands. But Schleiermacher has no hesitation in speaking of the divine *activity*, or of the one divine act, provided it is not thought of as resembling the individual and temporal acts of human activity. And it would surely be true to his intention if we concluded that every natural event is for him an act of God in the sense that it is grounded in the eternal activity of God.

It follows—again, strictly speaking—that no event is either more or less an act of God, or an effect of omnipotence, than any other event. Each event is woven inextricably into the total web of things, which is what it is by virtue of the divine good pleasure. But it does *not* follow that there cannot be events in which God is definitively revealed, that is to say, revealed in a way that defines God's nature for us. If we refer back to Schleiermacher's analogy of the human ego, we can surely say that of the hundred and one things a person does in the span of a lifetime, or even in the space of twenty-four hours, some things may stand out and furnish the key to everything else, unlocking the mystery of the person's true character. "Revelation" is the religious name for this kind of event, if what is disclosed is nothing less than the nature of things as grounded in omnipotent love. The name does not denote a special, particular act of God, for there *are* none, but an act or event that is especially revealing, an intimation of what the world is really like. "What is revelation?" Schleiermacher asks in the *Speeches on Religion*, and he answers: "Every original and new communication of the Universe to man is a revelation."

In terms of the story and the question with which I began, Schleiermacher might say something like this: We live in a world in which antennas fall because high winds blow and even top-grade metal gets fatigued. Nothing more needs to be said in explanation of falling antennas than just that. We would be remiss, however, if we did not also affirm that we live in a world in which persons are nurtured and cherished by the love of God. Any event may become an occasion by which this affirmation is elicited from us, but some events may be more effective than others. And experience shows that nothing brings home to us the question of meaning and purpose in our life more effectively than a happy escape from some disaster. A near miss invites a reappraisal of my goals; it confronts me with the fact that life is bounded by death, that there is an urgency about my decision concerning what to do with my allotted time. In the mind of someone who has acquired the art of "prayer without ceasing," why should the fall of an antenna—and contemplation on what it could have done but did not do—not become an occasion that stirs both the question of meaning and the affirmation of divine care?

In this light, we could perhaps put a sympathetic construction on the statement that "Somebody Up There is watching over us," though we might prefer to say more cautiously, "It is *as if* Somebody Up There were watching over us." Even Robert Lyde, our English mariner, was not mistaken in feeling that he lived in a world saturated with divine activity. We should wish to correct him, not for his lively sense of the presence of God, but for a very limited notion of God's purposes.

Naturally, the question must be asked: How is a duly corrected sense of the presence of God to be maintained when the course of events gives occasions to doubt it? Schleiermacher's answer, of course, is that a sense of God's presence is maintained through the person of the Savior, since the unique strength of his God-consciousness consisted precisely in his ability to bring the thought of God into relation with *everything* that happened to him—including the darkest moments of his suffering. Awareness of God is open in principle to all, simply by reason of everyone's humanity. But for the Christian everything is brought into relationship with the redemption accomplished by Jesus of Nazareth. Indeed, although every person is the object of divine love, the common God-consciousness does not, according to Schleiermacher, include an awareness of God's love. In *The Christian Faith* he says:

> By virtue of their capacity for consciousness of God, all men and women are also objects of the divine love. But the divine love is not for this reason realized in all. At most, they advance from fear of God—the dominant religious affection under the law— to the negative consciousness that the supreme being is not envious, and that is still far removed from a recognition of the divine love. Recognition of the divine love arises only with the activity of redemption and from Christ.

In conclusion, we are brought back once more to the unity of the general consciousness of God and the specific relation to Christ that Schleiermacher found in every Christian consciousness. Here, too, it is impossible to claim that he provides a definitive solution to a theological problem. Questions remain. But at least it is clear that the advance of scientific thought does not damage his notion of God-consciousness as it did the notion of a God who invades the world from the outside. Here, too, he made a fundamental theological move that was to have, and still does have, fruitful theological consequences. It is the direction he took, more than the conclusions he reached, that makes him the father of modern theology.

Moreover, his determination to hold together the two elements in the Christian consciousness remains paradigmatic, as it was in his day. As a Christian theologian, Schleiermacher would not permit either the substitution of a general philosophical theology for a specifically Christian dogmatics or a retreat from God-talk to a purely human and moral Jesus. "There can be no relation to Christ in which there is not also a relation to God . . . [and] within the Christian community there is no religious moment in which a relation to Christ is not also present with it." It is the careful balance of these two claims that makes Schleiermacher preeminently a church theologian—a prince of the church.

Sources

I have dispensed with any detailed apparatus of references to primary sources and secondary literature, indicating in this note only the sources of my direct quotations or allusions. Except for Frederica Rowan's translations, I have used my own English renderings throughout. Even so, I have thought it more useful in an introductory sketch of this kind to give references, wherever possible, to the corresponding passages in readily available English translations, rather than to the German originals I have actually used. Where a series of page numbers is given, it follows the order of my references (including specific allusions as well as actual quotations) in the lectures. Those who so wish should have no difficulty in finding the passages in the original texts for themselves.

The epigraph at the beginning of the book is from section nine of the *Brief Outline*; compare the English version in Friedrich Schleiermacher, *Brief Outline on the Study of Theology*, translated from the second German edition (1830) by Terrence N. Tice (Richmond: John Knox Press, 1966), p. 21.

1. RELIGION AND REFLECTION

The second edition (1827) of the Christmas dialogue has appeared in a new English version: Friedrich Schleiermacher, *Christmas Eve: Dialogue on the Incarnation*, trans. Terrence N. Tice (Richmond: John Knox Press, 1967). Much of the other primary material for the first lecture comes from Schleiermacher's speeches and letters. The third edition (1821) of the *Speeches on Religion*, as they are commonly titled, appeared in an English translation (1894) that has been reprinted: Friedrich Schleiermacher, *On Religion: Speeches to its Cultured Despisers*, trans. John Oman (New York: Harper & Brothers,

1958). See pp. 87–91 (on religion and doctrines); p. 9 (on Schleiermacher's religious upbringing); and pp. 12, 37, 47 (on feminine nature). The correspondence between Schleiermacher, his parents, and others is taken from the first volume of Frederica Rowan, trans., *The Life of Schleiermacher as Unfolded in His Autobiography and Letters*, 2 vols. (London: Smith, Elder, 1860), which also contains the report by Claus Harms and Schleiermacher's brief autobiographical statement. See pp. xvi, 25, 35, 4, 46, 53, 95, and 283–84. Friedrich Schlegel's recommendation that Schleiermacher should write a novel is noted in a letter on p. 223. I have occasionally made slight changes in Rowan's punctuation and have eliminated her use of the second person singular "thou," "thee," and "thy."

Schleiermacher's ideas concerning the practical, churchly character of theology are spelled out in the *Brief Outline*, but in addition I have alluded to a remark in his letters to Friedrich Lücke (1829). See Friedrich Schleiermacher, *On the Glaubenslehre: Two Letters to Dr. Lücke*, trans. James Duke and Francis S. Fiorenza, American Academy of Religion, Texts and Translations Series, no. 3 (Chico, Calif.: Scholars Press, 1981), p. 80. It is also in these open letters that he describes his theological enterprise as "empirical" (p. 45) and asks the rhetorical question cited in the last paragraph of the first lecture (pp. 40–41). Other writings by Schleiermacher referred to in the first lecture are the *Hermeneutics* and the *Sermons*. The posthumous *Hermeneutics* has only recently been translated into English: Friedrich Schleiermacher, *Hermeneutics: The Handwritten Manuscripts*, ed. Heinz Kimmerle, trans. James Duke and Jack Forstman, American Academy of Religion, Texts and Translations Series, no. 1 (Missoula, Mont.: Scholars Press, 1977). Schleiermacher's sermon on Eph. 5:22–31 is in *Selected Sermons of Schleiermacher*, trans. Mary F. Wilson (London: Hodder & Stoughton, 1890), pp. 130–46.

The first lecture mentions interpretations of Schleiermacher by Karl Barth, A. E. Biedermann, George Park Fisher, and

Ernst Troeltsch. Most of the references to Barth's thoughts on Schleiermacher are drawn from an essay of his that has been translated by George Hunsinger as "Concluding Unscientific Postscript on Schleiermacher" in *Studies in Religion/Sciences Religieuses* 7 (1978): 117–35, reprinted in Karl Barth, *The Theology of Schleiermacher: Lectures at Göttingen, Winter Semester of 1923/24*, ed. Dietrich Ritschl, trans. Geoffrey W. Bromiley (Grand Rapids, Mich.: Wm. B. Eerdmans, 1982), pp. 261–79. But the Niagara Falls simile appears in Barth's review of Brunner's book on Schleiermacher in *Zwischen den Zeiten* 2 [1924]: 49–64, untranslated as far as I know. This is the book Barth alludes to in his remark about "premises free from Schleiermacher." The remark can be found in Barth's *Protestant Theology in the Nineteenth Century: Its Background and History* (Valley Forge, Pa: Judson Press, 1973), p. 426. Biedermann's appraisal of Schleiermacher, also untranslated, is from a memorial address in his *Ausgewählte Vorträge und Aufsätze*, ed. J. Kradolfer (Berlin: Georg Reimer, 1885), pp. 186–210. Fisher's *History of Christian Doctrine* was published in the International Theological Library series (Edinburgh: T. & T. Clark, 1896). Troeltsch writes of the "technical-theological" character of Schleiermacher's dogmatics in his contribution to *Schleiermacher der Philosoph des Glaubens* (Berlin-Schöneberg: Buchverlag der "Hilfe," 1910), which contains essays by Troeltsch and others. Like Barth's review and Biedermann's memorial address, it is unfortunately not available in English.

2. THE CHRIST OF FAITH

The discussion in lecture two draws mostly from Schleiermacher's dogmatics. See Friedrich Schleiermacher, *The Christian Faith*, translated from the second German edition (1830-31), ed. H.R. Mackintosh and J. S. Stewart (Philadelphia: Fortress Press, 1976), pp. 427, 363, 52, 68, 390, 396, 397, 396, 396, 391, 394–95, 358–65 (cf. 747–48, on the dogma of the Trinity),

68, 375, 427, 363 (cf. 68–69), 492, 490–91 (cf. 77), 467, 425, 92, 377, 386–87. With my references to the *Speeches on Religion*, compare Oman's translation, pp. 2, 21 (cf. 37–38), 39, 141, 217, 223–24, 252, 246, 248, 250, 251, 248, 263–64; and with my references to the letters to Lücke, compare Duke and Fiorenza, *Two Letters to Dr. Lücke*, pp. 63–64, 41, 49. Schleiermacher's lectures on the life of Jesus, delivered in 1832, have been translated by S. Maclean Gilmour from the text published by K. A. Rütenik in 1864 and are included in the Life of Jesus Series, edited by Leander E. Keck. See Friedrich Schleiermacher, *The Life of Jesus* (Philadelphia: Fortress Press, 1975), with an introduction by Jack C. Verheyden; see especially p. 93.

A translation of Strauss's critique of Schleiermacher's lectures (1865) also appears in the Life of Jesus Series. See David Friedrich Strauss, *The Christ of Faith and the Jesus of History: A Critique of Schleiermacher's Life of Jesus*, trans. Leander E. Keck (Philadelphia: Fortress Press, 1977); see especially pp. 4, 35. Alexander Schweizer's perceptive remark, that it was Schleiermacher who led the Christian consciousness back to confidence in its own content, will be found in his untranslated work *Die protestantischen Centraldogmen in ihrer Entwicklung innerhalb der reformirten Kirche*, 2 vols. (Zurich: Orell, Füssli, 1854–56), 2:812.

3. THE ACTS OF GOD

In lecture three also, I have used mainly Schleiermacher's *The Christian Faith*. See the translation edited by Mackintosh and Stewart, pp. 749, 174, 261, 131–33, 17, 13, 206, 139, 148, 182 n.1, 215, 181, 171, 139, 203, 219, 501, 427–28, 137–38, 179, 730–31, 183, 735, 152, 501–2, 234, 558, 723–32, 50, 729, 131–32. See also Schleiermacher's *Speeches on Religion*, trans. Oman, pp. 92–99, 115–16, 89, and *Two Letters to Dr. Lücke*, trans. by Duke and Fiorenza, p. 40.

The fascinating sermon "On the Power of Prayer in Relation to Outward Circumstances," which appeared in an early collection of Schleiermacher's sermons (1801), is the first selection in Wilson's *Selected Sermons of Schleiermacher*, pp. 38–51. The correspondence between Schleiermacher and F. S. G. Sack has not been translated; the German texts will be found in Ludwig Jonas and Wilhelm Dilthey, eds., *Aus Schleiermacher's Leben: In Briefen*, 4 vols. (Berlin: Georg Reimer, 1858–63), 3:275–86.

For Richard R. Niebuhr's application of the term "Christomorphic" to Schleiermacher's dogmatics, see his book *Schleiermacher on Christ and Religion: A New Introduction* (New York: Charles Scribner's Sons, 1964), p. 212.

Index

Anselm, 50
Aquinas, Thomas, 20
Art, 44, 45
Atheism controversy, 59
Augsburg Confession, 39
Augustine, 20

Barth, Karl, 13, 14, 19, 20, 21, 22, 26
Biedermann, Alois Emanuel, 32
Brunner, Emil, 20
Bultmann, Rudolf, 22
Bunyan, John, 55

Calvin, John, 13, 18, 20, 22, 23, 29
Celebration of Christmas: A Conversation ("Christmas dialogue"), 27–31, 44, 46
Childhood, simplicity of, 28, 30, 31, 47
Christ: God-consciousness of, 48, 49, 50, 53, 69; redemption through, 35, 37, 38, 41, 43, 47, 48, 53, 54, 69; relation with, in Christian consciousness, 23, 35, 53, 69, 70; revelation in, 41, 54; two natures of, 39, 40, 41, 50, 52, 53
Christian Doctrine of Justification and Reconciliation, 19
Christian Faith, 18, 19, 26, 35, 37, 38, 44, 47, 49, 50, 51, 62, 64, 66, 69
Christianity, and other religions, 37, 41, 42, 45

Christology, 11, 23, 35–50, 52, 53, 60
Community, role of in theology, 35, 46, 47
Consciousness: religious, 44, 45, 64; religious character of human, 44, 60
Criticism, historical, 42

Deism, 41, 42, 45, 57, 58, 59
Dialogues Concerning Natural Religion, 58, 59
Dilthey, Wilhelm, 26

Enlightenment and Age of Reason, 39, 43, 44, 50, 54
Evangelical, 32, 33, 36; liberal, 31, 32, 33

Farmer, Herbert H., 14
Faust, 29
"Feeling of absolute dependence," 18, 60
Feelings, religious and intellectual reflection, relation of, 26, 27, 31, 32, 33, 35, 46, 47, 60
Feminine, 29, 47
Fisher, George Park, 31

God: acts of, 51–70; as artificer, 57, 58, 59; -consciousness, 23, 51, 53, 54, 58, 60, 61, 65, 66, 67, 69; as ground of being, 61; as highest unity, 62; love of, 67, 68, 69; as person, 62, 63, 64; proofs of, 59; as "Somebody Up There,"

61, 63, 64, 68;
"God-talk," problem of, 60
Goethe, Johann Wolfgang von,
  29, 59
Gospels, reliability of,
  30, 42, 47, 49, 50, 53
*Grace Abounding to the Chief
  of Sinners*, 55

Halle, University of, 26, 36
Harms, Claus, 17, 19
Hermeneutics, 23
History of Christian Doctrine
  (Fisher), 31
Hume, David, 58, 59

Institutes, 18
Isaiah, 61

James, William, 55, 56
Jesus, historical, 30, 42, 43, 47
Justin Martyr, 41

Lessing, Gotthold E., 42
Liberalism, theological, 13, 22
Life of Jesus (Schleiermacher),
  49
Lücke, Friedrich, 37, 49, 54
Luther, Martin, 13, 20, 22, 23,
  29, 33, 39, 43

Marriage and family, 29
Mediation, idea of, 46, 48
Moravian Brethren, 24, 25, 26,
  32, 35, 36
Music, as medium of religious
  expression, 28, 30, 31, 47

Natural Theology, 59
Nature, laws of, 57, 58, 64
Neo-orthodoxy, 13, 22
*New Hypothesis Concerning the
  Evangelists Regarded as Purely
  Human Historians*, 42

Newton, Isaac, 57
Niebuhr, Richard R., 53

*On Religion: Speeches to its
  Cultured Despisers.* See
  Speeches on Religion

Paley, William, 59
Pantheism, 59, 60, 62, 63;
  controversy, 59
Pauck, Wilhelm, 14
Pietism, 24, 26, 31, 32, 47
Piety, as object of theological re-
  flection, 31, 32, 43, 44, 46, 49
Prayer, 65, 66, 68
Preaching, 20, 38, 39, 42, 48
Predestination, 57
Principia Mathematica, 57
Providence, 57
Puritans, 55, 57

Reflection, 17, 27, 31, 35, 46
Reformation, 21, 33, 39;
  heritage, 21, 22, 39
Reimarus, Hermann Samuel, 42,
  43
Religion: essence of, 18, 27; as
  pious feeling, 18, 26, 27, 31,
  54; of reason, 41, 42, 45; as
  sense of infinite, 45
Revelation, 22, 67, 68; original,
  54
Ritschl, Albrecht, 19

Sack, Friedrich Samuel
  Gottfried, 62
Science and religion, problem
  of, 57, 59, 64, 65, 69
Schleiermacher, Friedrich:
  childhood and youth, 24–26,
  36; and Christ, relationship
  with, 24, 25, 26, 35, 36, 37,
  44; as church theologian, 20,
  21, 23, 70; and doctrine of

God, 60; and dogmas, role of in his thought, 36, 37, 38, 39, 40, 43, 52, 60; as empirical theologian, 21; as father of modern theology, 11, 21, 22, 43, 44, 69; as liberal evangelical, 31, 32, 33; marriage of, 30; as "Moravian of a higher order," 27, 32, 36, 37; as preacher, 12, 21, 62, 65; as "prince of the church," 12, 70; and Reformation heritage, loyalty to, 21, 23, 39; skepticism of, 24, 25, 26; as theological giant, 20; theology of, experiental character of, 21, 23, 31, 36, 37, 38, 46, 49, 53, 54, 60; and women, relationship with, 29, 30
Schweizer, Alexander, 44
Smith, Walter Chalmers, 61
Socinianism, 39

Speeches on Religion, 17, 18, 19, 23, 27, 29, 44, 46, 47, 62, 63, 68
Spinoza, Benedict, 59
Strauss, David Friedrich, 35, 37, 38, 53

Tertullian, 40
Theology: as concrete religious experience, 21, 22, 23; of the Holy Spirit, 22
Tillich, Paul, 61
Trinity, 38, 39, 40, 43
Troeltsch, Ernst, 21

Varieties of Religious Experience, 55

Wolfenbüttel Fragments, 42
Womanhood, 28, 29, 30, 31
Word of God and the Word of Man, 13